Love Bears All Things
A Child Learns to Love

"Love . . . bears all things."
I Corinthians 13:7

All of us want our own children, as well as the other children we know and care for, to understand the concept of love and to show love in everyday behavior. I Corinthians 13, the great love chapter of the Bible, tells us how love acts and behaves. *Love Bears All Things* will help you teach these key behaviors to your children.

A BEAR HUGS BOOK ™

Love Bears All Things: A Child Learns to Love

Bear Up: A Child Learns to Handle Ups and Downs

Bearing Burdens: A Child Learns to Help

Bear Buddies: A Child Learns to Make Friends

Bearing Fruit: A Child Learns About the Fruit of the Spirit

I Can Bearly Wait: A Child Learns Patience

Titles in Preparation:

Bears Repeating: A Child Learns Thankfulness

You are Beary Special: A Child Learns Self-esteem

Bear Necessities: A Child Learns Obedience

Bear Facts: A Child Learns Truthfulness

Bearing Good News: A Child Learns to Be Positive

Sweeter Than Honey: A Child Learns the Golden Rule

Copyright 1986, Paul C. Brownlow
Hardcover, ISBN: 0-915720-50-7
Library Edition, ISBN: 0-915720-61-2

Brownlow Publishing Company, Inc.
6309 Airport Freeway, Fort Worth, Texas 76117

Love Bears All Things
A Child Learns to Love

By

Pat Kirk & Alice Brown

Illustrated by

Diann Bartnick

BROWNLOW PUBLISHING COMPANY, INC.

Make life "bearable." Live your life
stuffed with as much love as you can.
Then, give away as much as you can.

You won't get skinny and everyone
will feel full of good things, too!
Here are some "bear facts" about love.

Love is patient

Love keeps working instead of crying.

Love faces those laces and keeps on trying.

Love is kind

Love is friendly to the new bear at school.
Love lives by the Golden Rule:

"If I were new, just like you,
I would need a good friend, too."

Love is not jealous, not boastful

Love can still grin from ear to ear

when someone else gets all the cheers!

Love is not proud

Love never acts proud and sasses,

"I'm first! You're last!"

Love knows that others

are also thirsty in the class.

Love is not rude

Love doesn't trip others just for fun.

Fun that hurts others must not be done!

Love is not selfish

Love will take a piggy bank

to buy our mother a china plate.

Love is not angered easily

Love knows that even a
    birthday toy can get broken.

Tantrums can't replace it.

Love is soft-spoken.

Love does not remember wrongs

Love says, "You did your best
at baking a cake.

You'll do better next time.
We all make mistakes."

Love is not happy with evil

Love never cheats to beat.

Play by the rules.

That's the way to compete.

Love is happy with truth

Love returns something lost
to the right place.

"Finders keepers, losers weepers"
is not one of love's ways.

Love patiently accepts all things

Love is a treat to all!

The big, the small, the short, the tall!

Love always trusts, always hopes

Love can win and love can lose.

Love knows how it feels

to walk in someone else's shoes.

Love continues strong

Love is not stingy with big bear hugs.
Everyone needs to give and get love.

Aren't we thankful to God—
for loving us every day
and showing us love's way?

Let's love God back—
by showing our love for
ourselves, our families and friends.

Then life will always be full of love
and happiness will never end.